DOS
Essentials

Rod B. Southworth

bf

boyd & fraser publishing company

CREDITS:

Publisher: Tom Walker
Acquisitions Editor: James H. Edwards
Production Coordinator: Pat Donegan
Manufacturing Director: Dean Sherman
Composition and Interior Design: Gex, Inc.
Cover Illustration and Design: Susan Yousem

bf ©1991 by boyd & fraser publishing company
A Division of South-Western Publishing Company
Boston, MA 02116

Manufactured in the United States of America

DOS is a registered trademark of IBM Corporation.
MS-DOS is a registered trademark of Microsoft Corporation.
PC-DOS is a registered trademark of IBM Corporation.

Library of Congress Cataloging-in-Publication Data

Southworth, Rod B., 1941-
    DOS essentials / Rod B. Southworth.
        p.   cm.
    Includes index.
    ISBN 0-87835-690-8
    1. PC DOS (Computer operating system) 2. MS-DOS (Computer
operating system)   I. Title.
QA76.76.063S6593   1991
005.4'46--dc20   90-23930
                                                            CIP

    2 3 4 5 6 7 8 9 10 M 4 3 2 1

Contents

Preface

DOS Essentials is ideally suited for use in any formal educational or training environment, or for self-study. It is designed for use as a supplementary text in any microcomputer course.

OBJECTIVES OF THIS BOOK

The objectives of this book are:

- To introduce readers to the concepts of operating systems.
- To guide novice users through the process of learning just the essential DOS commands and concepts needed to run applications.
- To simplify the use of high-frequency DOS commands and associated options.

DISTINGUISHING FEATURES

Simplifies Using DOS

Topics in this book are introduced in a logical step-by-step manner, as they are needed for application by the student. By building on students' prior experience and carefully constructed examples of DOS in action, this simplified approach helps readers become self-sufficient microcomputer users.

Focus on High-Frequency DOS Commands

This textbook features step-by-step instruction in using DOS 3.3 commands and options that are most frequently required by microcomputer users. Specific concepts like filenames, system defaults, and use of wildcard characters are introduced as needed. It is designed to help readers gain a better understanding and control of using microcomputers as a tool.

Floppy Disk and Hard Disk Environments

In keeping with the current trend in microcomputer instruction, this book consistently addresses the use of DOS in both floppy disk and hard disk environments. A separate set of exercises is included for at the end of each chapter.

Class-Tested Review Questions and Exercises

Each chapter has a substantial set of review questions and student exercises that have been class-tested over the last three years. The exercises build on material learned from previous chapters, as well as reinforce the new material from each chapter.

Actual Screen Illustrations

DOS commands and exercises are supported with screen "dumps" that accurately reflect what user's screens will look like as they execute each target command. The screen illustrations provide users with visual verification, which highlights the impact of each operation performed.

Proven Material

This text is based on many semesters of teaching DOS and on the collective experience of the instructors and students who have shared their comments and suggestions. Every attempt has been made to preserve the integrity of those elements that proved effective and to improve on those that did not.

Instructor's Support Material

An Instructor's Manual features an introduction to microcomputers, supplemental information on DOS, and answers to the review questions. Students with no previous understanding of microcomputers should be given a brief introduction to using microcomputers, including the keyboard, prior to beginning the first chapter. The Instructor's Manual is available to adopters of this text. Instructors may contact South-Western Publishing Company to obtain this supplementary material.

ACKNOWLEDGMENTS

This book would not have been possible without the guidance, help, and advice of many supportive individuals. I would like to give my thanks to the following instructors who provided valuable suggestions during the development of this text: Patrice Gapen, Dick Krahenbuhl, Gary Sharp, and Cathy Stoughton, all from Laramie County Community College; and Dr. Lowell Barr and Debbie Ramirez from the University of Wyoming.

The entire staff at boyd & fraser, especially Pat Donegan and Jim Edwards, did a remarkable job of editing and producing this text. I remain indebted to all my contributors for their efforts on my behalf.

Rod B. Southworth   January 3, 1991
Cheyenne, Wyoming   CompuServe 71210,1546

Overview of DOS

All computer systems require an operating system to direct the activities of the hardware. The primary objective of Chapter 1 is to introduce you to the Disk Operating System (DOS), used by most microcomputer systems. Additionally, Chapter 1 teaches you the basic functions related to file management and command processing. This overview provides the necessary foundation to help you understand and use the DOS commands explained in this text. Specifically, you will learn the major parts of DOS, understand how files are saved on disks, know the difference between internal and external DOS commands, and begin using DOS by booting the system.

INTRODUCTION TO DOS

An operating system is an integral part of all computer systems. It allows users like you to conveniently use the computer as a tool. For example, suppose you wanted to use your computer to create a term paper with a new word-processing program. You would have to know how to load and execute the correct program. In addition, each application has to know how to save and retrieve disk files on your disk. This is all accomplished by the computer's disk operating system, called **DOS**.

DOS is the translator between the hardware and software. It coordinates and controls all the activities of the computer (see Figure 1-1). DOS contains a group of commands and programs that allow users to interact directly with the computer. For example, it provides an easy way to copy data from one disk to another, allowing you to conveniently make a duplicate, or backup copy, of important data.

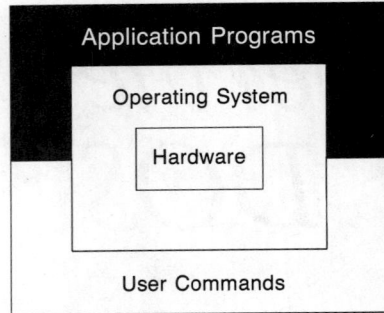

Figure 1-1
The Role of an Operating System.

Application Programs

Operating System

Hardware

User Commands

This chapter introduces you to a specific type of disk operating system called **PC-DOS** (or **MS-DOS**), which is used on both IBM and IBM-compatible microcomputers. The two operating systems are very similar and can be used on all IBM-compatible microcomputers. PC-DOS is IBM's DOS and MS-DOS is Microsoft's version. Because of the similarities of PC-DOS and MS-DOS, this text refers to both operating systems simply as DOS.

BASIC DOS FUNCTIONS
DOS has three major functions. It controls the input and output operations of your computer. The second function interprets and executes commands you enter from your keyboard or other input devices. File management, the last function of DOS, allows you to permanently save files on disks and organize them effectively.

Control Input/Output Operations

All application programs share the same input and output problems. They all have to accept data from the keyboard, display data on the monitor, store data temporarily in main memory, store data permanently on disk, and retrieve data from disks. These functions require a great number of instructions to coordinate and control all these activities on a microcomputer. Without an operating system, each application, such as a word processing or payroll program, would have to duplicate these instructions.

Interpret and Execute Commands

The command processor part of DOS interprets and executes the commands you enter. Without an operating system, you would have no effective way to communicate with the hardware and direct its activities.

File Management

Computer users are heavily involved with the file management role of DOS. For example, sometimes you need to list, save, rename, copy, or delete files on a disk. DOS provides a series of commands to allow both the user and application programs to manage the multitude of disk files that are created over a period of time.

SAVING FILES WITH DOS
A **file** is a group of related records, where each record consists of an organized group of characters. **Records** are saved as part of a file. Records consist of either program instructions or data. Thus, files are categorized as either program files or data files.

Because the files you create and work with in main memory are temporary, the ability to save files on disk is a requirement of all operating systems. Files become permanent only when you save them on disk. When you turn off the computer or otherwise lose power to main memory, everything in main memory is destroyed. DOS does not save files automatically. However, you can duplicate files by using the COPY command, covered in Chapter 3.

Although it appears to be a fairly simple process, DOS goes through a number of important steps to save files. The following overview explains this process.

1. Before a disk can be used to store data, it must be specifically formatted by the operating system. The FORMAT command is used to properly define the areas on the disk for recording data. When you issue a save command from an application program or directly from DOS, the operating system reads the directory portion of the disk to determine a suitable location to save the file.

2. If the file being saved is a new file, DOS tries to locate enough empty space to hold the file. If the file was previously saved on that disk, DOS replaces the contents of the old file on the disk with the contents of the file currently in main memory. Because DOS uses whatever areas it can find to save the data, the locations may not be adjoining. Files written in noncontiguous locations are called **fragmented files**. The additional disk head movement caused by fragmentation may slow down the reading and writing of these files considerably.

3. When a file has been saved, DOS updates a special area on the disk with system information. This information is used by DOS to create a directory listing of files on a disk and to retrieve files when needed. This reserved area on disk is covered further during the explanation of the FORMAT command in Chapter 2.

MAJOR DOS PARTS

Before a DOS command can be executed, it must be loaded into the main memory of the CPU. Main memory is also called **random-access memory**, or **RAM**. Because DOS is too large to reside in RAM at one time, DOS commands are subdivided into two parts: the RAM-resident portion, which always resides in RAM, and a set of utility programs that remain on disk until they are needed. The RAM-resident portion is initially loaded into RAM when the computer is first turned on. Figure 1-2 provides an overview of the major parts of DOS.

Figure 1-2
Major Parts of DOS.

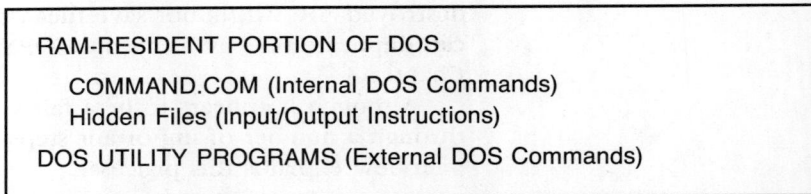

RAM-RESIDENT PORTION OF DOS

    COMMAND.COM (Internal DOS Commands)
    Hidden Files (Input/Output Instructions)

DOS UTILITY PROGRAMS (External DOS Commands)

RAM-Resident Portion of DOS

The RAM-resident portion of DOS is made up of three specific files: the **COMMAND.COM** file, and two DOS system files. The COMMAND.COM file contains DOS commands that are most often used. Because they are stored in RAM they are referred to as internal DOS commands. These commands let you list the filenames stored on a disk and let you copy, view, and delete files. The two system files are used by DOS to translate general operating system commands into the specific input/output instructions required by your computer hardware. When you list the files contained on your DOS disk, these two system files do not appear on the directory of files. Therefore, they are called **hidden files**.

Utility Programs

Whereas most of the common DOS commands are grouped into a single file (COMMAND.COM), the remaining DOS commands are stored in individual disk files, referred to as DOS **utility programs**. These programs (external commands) are only loaded into RAM when they are needed. For example, the program used to format your disks (FORMAT.COM), is loaded into RAM only when it is being executed.

BOOTING DOS
Before you can use an operating system, you must load it from a secondary storage device, such as a disk, to the main memory of the computer. Because not all parts of the operating system can be loaded at once, a process known as **booting the system** is used to load the controlling portion of the operating system. With hard disk systems, DOS looks for the DOS system files on the hard disk rather than a floppy disk drive.

There are two general methods of booting any operating system. One method is called a **cold boot**, because the computer is turned off prior to booting the operating system. The second method is termed a **warm boot** because the computer is already warmed up and was previously in use, but needs to be rebooted. In both cases, DOS goes through the same process.

Cold Boot

Experience has shown that people learn best by doing. So go ahead and follow these steps to do a cold boot of DOS from a floppy disk. If you have a hard disk system, skip the first step and change all references of Drive A to Drive C.

1. Place the disk containing DOS in Drive A with the latch securely closed. Drive A is usually either the top drive or left-most drive in microcomputers with two drives.

2. Turn on the power to both the monitor and the CPU.

3. The microcomputer begins executing a small startup program permanently stored in the CPU, which instructs it to do some diagnostic testing. The tests include checking the computer's RAM and keyboard interface to make sure they are functional. If there are any problems, the program displays an appropriate error message on your screen.

4. If the computer passes the diagnostic checks, the startup program loads the two DOS hidden files contained on the DOS disk in Drive A. It also loads the COMMAND.COM file into

RAM from Drive A. The COMMAND.COM file contains many of the DOS commands you will use. It is also responsible for interpreting and executing your commands. If you're working with a hard disk system, these system files will be retrieved from the hard disk.

5. With floppy disk systems and some hard disk systems, DOS asks you to enter the correct date and time, so it can keep track of the time with its own clock. Once you've entered the date and time, DOS displays the version number of the operating system and prompts you to enter a command. The default prompt for a floppy disk system is A>, where the A represents the default disk drive, the one containing the DOS disk. Figure 1-3 shows you how the screen might look if you entered a date of July 4, 1990 and a time of 1:45 P.M. A> is the system prompt, which requests the next command. The underline character following A> represents the cursor on the screen. For illustrative purposes, the data you entered is shown in boldface.

Figure 1-3
Screen Display after Booting PC-DOS.

```
Current date is Tue 1-01-1980
Enter new date (mm-dd-yy): 07-04-90
Current time is 0:01.05.58
Enter new time: 13:45
The IBM Personal Computer DOS
Vers. 3.10 (C)Copyright International Business
            Machines 1981, 1985
            (C)Copyright Microsoft Corp. 1981, 1985

A>_
```

The system date is entered using month, day, and year in the form of mm-dd-yy or mm/dd/yy. You can use either a slash (/), a hyphen (-), or a period (.) to separate the date entries.

The system time is entered using hours, minutes, and seconds in the form of hh:mm:ss. The use of seconds (ss) is optional. Hours are always entered using the 24-hour system and range from 0 to 23. You can only use a colon (:) or period (.) to separate time entries.

As with most operating systems, when you finish entering a command or data, such as the date or time, you need to press the Enter key to let the system know you're finished keying.

As long as DOS continues running, it keeps track of the time, automatically changing both the time and the date. Many systems today have a small battery and additional software to keep track of the date and time when the computer is turned off. When the system is booted, the system date and time can be set automatically from this clock.

Warm Boot

The major difference between the two booting methods is in how the boot process is initiated. In a cold boot, the computer is simply turned on to initiate the booting process. With a warm boot the power is already on. It is advisable to use a warm boot whenever you can to minimize the possibility of damaging the electronic chips when the power is turned on. A warm boot is activated by pressing three keys simultaneously: the Control key, the Alternate key, and the Delete key. This combination of keystrokes is shown as Ctrl-Alt-Del. To do a warm boot, press the Ctrl and Alt keys with your left hand, lightly touch the Del key with your right hand, and release all three keys.

TYPES OF DOS COMMANDS Because the full set
of DOS commands is too extensive to be completely loaded into RAM, some commands are initially loaded into RAM and others remain externally stored on the DOS disk until they are needed. DOS commands are classified as being either **internal** or **external commands**.

Internal Commands

The internal commands are contained in the COMMAND.COM file. Internal commands are available to DOS when the system is booted and a copy of the COMMAND.COM file is loaded into RAM. Because it is much faster to access commands from RAM, the designers of DOS chose the most commonly used commands to be internal.

Essential internal commands include DIR, TYPE and DEL. The DIR command is used to get a directory listing of files stored on a disk. The TYPE command is used to display the contents of non-executable files (i.e., MEMO.TXT) on the screen. And the DEL command allows you to delete unwanted files from a disk. These internal commands are covered in the next chapter.

External Commands

Because RAM must be used efficiently, external commands reside on the DOS disk as utility programs. They are only loaded into RAM when they are needed. The FORMAT command (Chapter 2) is an example of an external command.

SUMMARY OF NEW TERMS DOS is the disk operating system for IBM and IBM-compatible microcomputers. It consists of a set of system files stored on a disk, representing all of the commands needed to make the computer operate and run application programs. Three of the DOS files, COMMAND.COM and two hidden files, are copied into memory when the system is turned on, or booted. These are called RAM-resident files, because they remain in memory until the power is turned off. The COMMAND.COM file contains commonly used DOS *internal commands*. The hidden files (files that do not show on a directory listing) provide DOS with the input and output instructions needed to direct the hardware. Less common DOS *external commands* reside on the DOS disk as utility programs. They are copied into memory as they are needed. Before you can issue any commands to a computer, the controlling portion of the operating system must be loaded to memory. This process, known as booting the system, loads the RAM-resident DOS files (COMMAND.COM and the two hidden files), requests the system date and time, and displays the system prompt. You can begin issuing commands at the system prompt (A>). The term *warm boot* is used to describe the boot process when the computer is already turned on. Otherwise, the process is called a *cold boot*.

Review Questions

1. Why is an operating system necessary?
2. What does the term *DOS* mean?
3. Why are there two different types of DOS (MS-DOS and PC-DOS)?
4. What are the primary functions of DOS?
5. What does the term *RAM-resident* mean?
6. What is the function of the system information area of a disk?

7. What is an application program?

8. What is meant by the term *hidden files*?

9. What is the purpose of hidden files?

10. What is the purpose of the COMMAND.COM file?

11. What is meant by *booting the system*?

12. What happens to data in RAM when the power is turned off?

13. Why are some DOS commands referred to as *internal* and others *external*?

14. What type of commands are contained in the COMMAND.COM file?

15. What process must be done before files can be saved on a disk?

16. When you initiate a system boot, what happens after the diagnostic testing is completed?

17. What is the difference between a warm boot and a cold boot?

18. How do you activate a warm boot?

19. How would you enter a system date of February 14, 1991?

20. How would you enter a time of 2:35 PM?

LAB EXERCISE – FLOPPY DISK USERS

These exercises were developed for computers with two floppy disk drives. Drive A will contain your DOS disk and Drive B will be used for your data disk.

This first exercise has you do a warm boot; it assumes the system is already turned on from work done previously in the chapter. If it is not already on, do a cold boot of your system before proceeding.

• With the DOS disk in Drive A, use Ctrl-Alt-Del to boot DOS.

• Enter the current date in mm-dd-yy format (i.e., 4-15-91).

• Enter the correct time in hh:mm format (i.e., 11:07).

• Remember to press the Enter key (or Return) to cause the computer to act on your data.

This completes the first lab exercise. Remember to remove your floppy disks before you leave the computer. There are a variety of ways to leave your computer when you are finished, so ask your instructor how to exit your system.

LAB EXERCISE – HARD DISK USERS

These exercises were developed for computers with one hard disk and one floppy disk drive. Drive C will contain your DOS disk and Drive A will be used for your data disk.

This first exercise has you do a warm boot; it assumes the system is already turned on from work done previously in the chapter. If it is not already on, do a cold boot of your system before proceeding.

- Use Ctrl-Alt-Del to boot DOS.
- Enter the current date in mm-dd-yy format (i.e., 4-15-91).
- Enter the correct time in hh:mm format (i.e., 11:07).
- Remember to press the Enter key (or Return) to cause the computer to act on your data.

This completes the first lab exercise. Remember to remove your floppy disk before you leave the computer. There are a variety of ways to leave your computer when you are finished, so ask your instructor how to exit your system.

Beginning DOS Commands

The objective of Chapter 2 is to get you started using DOS. You will learn how to format a disk, change the system date and time, get a directory listing of files on a disk, display the contents of disk files, and erase files from a disk. Chapter 2 covers six essential DOS commands: FORMAT, DIR, DATE, TIME, TYPE, and DEL.

FORMATTING DISKS WITH DOS To save files on disk, the disk must be properly prepared to accept the data to be saved. When you purchase a new blank disk, it is a "generic" disk, which can be used with different operating systems. Therefore, each blank disk must be customized according to the requirements of DOS. This customizing process is called **formatting** a disk. It includes the following operations:

1. Formatting creates addressable areas of the disk where data can be stored. Because each disk drive and operating system have its own addressing scheme, this activity is mandatory prior to saving files. Each of the forty tracks on one side of most 5¼-inch low-density floppy disks is divided into nine sectors, for a total of 360 sectors per side. The term **cluster** is used to represent a corresponding track and sector on both sides of a disk. A cluster is the smallest addressable location on a disk. Because a sector holds 512 bytes of data, the typical cluster size is 1024 bytes.

2. Formatting checks every recording spot on the disk for damage, noting any clusters that are not acceptable for storing data.

3. Additionally, formatting creates a directory area and **File Allocation Table (FAT)** on the disk. These special areas are used by DOS to keep track of saved files. Any unacceptable disk clusters and the allocated locations of each file stored on the disk are recorded in the disk's FAT.

FORMAT Command

The **FORMAT** command is used to prepare a disk for use by DOS. When you format a disk, the system displays the status of your disk, including the total number of bad sectors it finds. DOS will not store anything in bad sectors. The following example shows the information displayed after the command FORMAT was entered and the disk being formatted had eight clusters with bad sectors:

        362496 bytes total disk space
          8192 bytes in bad sectors
        354304 bytes available on disk

The FORMAT command has several helpful options available. Command options are shown with brackets [ ] throughout the text. One option, the system option [/S], tells DOS to format the disk and include the DOS system programs (used to boot DOS) on the disk. When DOS formats a disk with the system option, it writes three files on the disk. Two of these are hidden, which means you cannot see them when you display a directory of the disk. The third file is the COMMAND.COM file, containing all the internal DOS commands. To use the system option and create a bootable disk on Drive B, enter FORMAT B: /S.

Another helpful option of the FORMAT command is the volume option [/V], which lets you name your disk with a volume label. You can create an "electronic" label of up to eleven characters for each disk. This label is especially helpful when working with numerous disks, because you can identify a disk without having to remove it from the drive. To use the volume label option to format a disk in Drive B, enter FORMAT B: /V. To use it with the system option, enter FORMAT B: /S/V (or FORMAT B: /V/S).

The FORMAT command also has options that can be used to format different sizes of floppy disks. Because these options tend to vary by type of DOS and hardware configuration used, you could consult your instructor for the proper options to use.

DEFAULT DISK DRIVE CONCEPT In many

instances DOS needs to know what disk drive applies to the commands you enter. It uses a **default drive approach**. Whenever you enter a command without a disk drive specification, DOS substitutes the default drive in its place. You specify which disk drive is to be the default drive. You can save a significant number of keystrokes when entering commands by understanding this concept. *You only need to specify a disk drive if it is other than the default drive*.

To identify the different disk drives, DOS uses a coding scheme consisting of a letter and a colon. A: and B: are used for floppy drives, while C: and D: are used to represent hard disk drives. DOS establishes the initial default drive as the disk drive that was used to boot the system: Drive A for floppy disk systems and Drive C for hard disk systems. You can easily change the default to another drive whenever you wish. When you boot DOS and see the A> prompt, the A refers to the default disk drive. The > is the symbol used as part of the DOS system prompt to let you know it is ready to receive a command from you.

To change the default drive, you need to enter a new disk drive letter followed by a colon. For example, the command B: entered at the A> prompt, changes the default disk. Once entered, the default drive becomes Drive B (the second floppy drive) and the system prompt is displayed as B>.

FILE NAMING CONVENTION
DOS uses all parts of the **filename** to tell it where to search for a specified file. The full filename consists of four parts: the disk drive containing the file, the path, the filename, and the filename extension. Brackets are used throughout the text to identify the parts of the full filename that are optional. Only the filename itself is required. The full filename is as follows:

`[d:][path]filename[.ext]`

The first part of the full filename, [d:], is used to specify the disk drive. To specify a drive, enter the drive letter followed by a colon. If you omit the drive designator, the default disk drive is substituted by DOS.

The next part, [path], represents the subdirectory containing the file. Discussion of this parameter is postponed until Chapter 4, when we discuss hard disk systems that use subdirectories.

DOS requires a filename that is from one to eight characters in length. Filenames can be made up of numeric digits, alphabetic letters, and certain special characters. You should avoid using any special characters, except hyphens (-), which can be used to make filenames more readable. DOS does not allow the use of spaces or punctuation, such as periods, commas, colons, or semicolons in filenames.

The final part of the full filename is an optional extension [.ext]. It is one to three characters long and uses the same set of characters valid for filenames. If an extension is used, it must be preceded by a period (i.e., A:JONES89.DOC). The purpose of a filename extension is to indicate the type of file. Using filename extensions is highly recommended to aid in keeping track of your files. For example, you can use .DOC, .WP, or .TXT for word processing files and .WK or .WKS for worksheet files.

When creating filenames, you should always use meaningful titles to further classify the data contained in each file. You can code a great deal of information into your filenames. For example, a set of memos on a new bottling plant could be named BOTTLE1.DOC, BOTTLE2.DOC, etc. If the memo dates were critical, they could be named BOTmmdd.DOC, where mmdd represents the month and day the file was created. When disk directories are displayed in filename sequence, the memos would appear listed together chronologically. As the number of files grows, the benefits of care and foresight in creating filenames becomes more significant.

When you assign file extensions, you should abide by the standard extensions already established and commonly used. Many of these standard extensions are included in Table 2-1.

Table 2-1
Standard Filename Extensions.

$$$	scratch or temporary file
BAK	backup file
BAS	BASIC program file (needs compiling first)
BAT	executable batch file (file of DOS commands)
COM	executable command file (machine language), type in the filename and press the Return key
DAT	data file (listable via the TYPE command)
DBF	dBASE III, III PLUS, or IV file
DEF	program definition or setup file
DOC	documentation file, similar to DAT
EXE	executable file, similar to COM file, but must be allocated to a specific memory location
MSG	message file, similar to DAT or DOC
OVL	overlay file (used by large programs)
PRN	printer file (can be modified prior to printing)
SYS	operating system file (like a device driver)
TXT	text file, similar to DAT, DOC, and MSG
WKS	Lotus 1-2-3 worksheet file

DISK DIRECTORY LISTING When you get a directory listing on your screen, DOS displays more than just the filenames. The file size in bytes (where one byte stores one character) and a **date stamp** is displayed for each file. The date stamp is the date and time each file was last changed on the disk. As the number of files increases, large, the correct date stamp becomes extremely useful. This is why it is important to enter the date and time correctly whenever DOS is booted. Figure 2-1 shows you a directory listing of a sample DOS disk.

```
A>DIR

  Volume in drive A is DOS33
  Directory of  A:\

COMMAND  COM    25532  10-31-88   2:54p
ANSI     SYS     1647   4-07-88   9:58a
ATTRIB   EXE    10656   4-07-88   7:42a
BACKUP   COM    29114  11-15-88   2:44p
CHKDSK   COM    11003   6-09-88   9:34a
DISKCOPY COM     6762   6-23-88  10:02a
EDLIN    COM     7495   6-02-88   2:06p
FORMAT   COM    12206   8-19-88   4:02p
LABEL    COM     2346   4-07-88   7:43a
PARK     COM    12068  11-09-84   8:53p
RESTORE  COM    26480  11-15-88   2:45p
SORT     EXE     1946   4-07-88   7:42a
SYS      COM     5045   6-14-88   3:45p
TREE     COM     2083   1-11-89  10:30a
XCOPY    EXE    11216   4-07-88   7:44a
       15 File(s)    135168 bytes free

A>
```

DIR (Directory) Command

`DIR [d:][filename[.ext]] [/P][/W]`

The **DIR** command displays a directory (listing) of the files on a specified disk. The information provided in the directory includes the volume label, the name of each file, the size in bytes of each file, the date and time each file was last saved, and the amount of free space left on the disk. Brackets are used throughout this text to indicate the command parts that are optional. For example, if you do not designate a disk drive [d:], DOS uses the default drive. If you specify an optional filename, the directory is limited to only listing that name.

Subdirectory names (covered in Chapter 4) are also displayed on the directory and are clearly identified with <DIR> in the file size field. Entries for the hidden system files are never listed, even when present.

Use the **/P** option to cause the computer to pause during the display of the directory when the screen is full. It continues displaying again after you press any key to signal you are ready to continue.

Use the **/W** option to display the directory in wide format, in which only the filenames are displayed across the screen, five files on a line. You can use the /W option to save display time and space. Figure 2-2 shows you what the wide format might look like.

Figure 2-2
Screen Display of DIR with Wide (/W) Option.

```
A>DIR /W

  Volume in drive A is DOS33
  Directory of  A:\

COMMAND  COM    ANSI     SYS    ATTRIB   EXE    BACKUP   COM    CHKDSK   COM
DISKCOPY COM    EDLIN    COM    FORMAT   COM    LABEL    COM    PARK     COM
RESTORE  COM    SORT     EXE    SYS      COM    TREE     COM    XCOPY    EXE
        15 File(s)     135168 bytes free

A>
```

When you enter DOS commands, the system automatically converts all lowercase characters to uppercase. To help you remember this helpful feature, the examples of usage in this text show DOS commands in varying combinations of upper and lower case.

Examples of Usage:

A> D I R (display directory of all files on the default disk drive)

A> D I R B: (display directory of all files in Drive B)

B> D i r (displays directory of all files on the default drive, B)

A> d i r b: /p (display the Drive B directory, pausing whenever the screen is full)

A> d i r /w (display filenames on the default drive in wide format)

A> DIR B:/W/P (display filenames on Drive B in wide format, pausing after each screen).

In the previous example, notice that the / acts as a delimiter, just like a space. Delimiters are used to separate the parts of a DOS command and make it easier for DOS to interpret commands correctly.

WILDCARD CHARACTERS

Wildcard characters have been appropriately named because, like jokers in a card game, they can be used to represent any characters in DOS commands. The wildcard character used most often by DOS is the asterisk (*), representing a group of characters.

The best way to understand the use of wildcard characters is by example. If you wish to display a directory listing of all the files on Drive A that begin with LTR and that have an extension of DOC, you could enter the following command: DIR A:LTR*.DOC. In this example, the asterisk substitutes for any group of characters, so that filenames LTRSMITH.DOC, LTR4.DOC, and LTRBILL3.DOC would all qualify to be displayed in the directory.

Wildcard characters can also be used with optional filename extensions. For example:

DIR A:TEXT.* (list all files on Drive A with a filename of TEXT, regardless of extension)

DIR B:P*.TR* /W (list in wide format any filename on Drive B starting with P and having an extension starting with TR)

Try the following examples using your DOS disk by entering the commands at the A> system prompt. (Note: If you are using a hard disk system, remember to replace all reference to Drive A in these examples with Drive C.) Remember that these commands may be entered using lowercase characters.

DIR (list all files on Drive A)

DIR A:*.EXE (list just those with an extension of .EXE)

DIR A:S*.* (list all files that begin with an S)

Figure 2-3 shows what the display screen might look like after executing the last two commands.

Figure 2-3

Screen Display of Using Wildcards.

```
A>DIR A:*.EXE

 Volume in drive A is DOS33
 Directory of  A:\

ATTRIB   EXE   10656   4-07-88   7:42a
SORT     EXE    1946   4-07-88   7:42a
XCOPY    EXE   11216   4-07-88   7:44a
        3 File(s)    135168 bytes free

A>DIR A:S*.*

 Volume in drive A is DOS33
 Directory of  A:\

SORT     EXE    1946   4-07-88   7:42a
SYS      COM    5045   6-14-88   3:45p
        2 File(s)    135168 bytes free

A>
```

MORE BEGINNING DOS COMMANDS

DATE Command

DATE [mm-dd-yy] -or- DATE [mm/dd/yy]

The **DATE** command lets you change the system date once the system is booted. If you specify a new date when you enter the command, it is changed immediately. If you omit this optional parameter, the system displays the current date and prompts you to enter a new date. Press the Enter key if you do not wish to change it. If you enter an invalid date, you are prompted to enter a correct date.

Examples of usage:
A> DATE 3/4/91 (changes the system date to March 4, 1991)

A> date 03-04-91 (changes the system date to March 4, 1991)

A> Date (displays the current date and prompts you to change it)

TIME Command

```
TIME [hh:mm[:ss]]
```

The **TIME** command is used to change the system time. Because hours are entered using a 24-hour clock, 1:00 P.M. is entered as 13:00. It is important to keep the correct date and time on the system because it is recorded in the directory information of each file you save. If you omit the optional parameters, the current system time is displayed and you are prompted to change it. To leave the time unchanged, just press the Enter key. If you enter an invalid time, the system prompts you to reenter a correct time.

Examples of usage:

A> TIME 8:30 (changes the system time to 8:30 A.M.)

A> time 14:15:35 (changes the time to 2:15 P.M. and 35 seconds)

A> time (displays the current time and prompts you to enter a new time)

DEL (Delete) Command

```
DEL [d:]filename[.ext]
```

The **DEL** command deletes the specified disk file. For example, to delete a file named MEMO.DOC on Drive B, you would enter the command DEL B:MEMO.DOC. If the drive designator is not specified, the default drive is assumed. You can use wildcard characters in the filename and extension, but do so with caution, as multiple files can quickly be deleted with a single command. If you use *.* to specify the file, all files on the designated disk will be deleted. When you attempt to delete all files on a disk, the DEL command gives you some measure of protection against eliminating files by mistake. It pauses to ask you if you are sure. You are not allowed to delete read-only files or DOS hidden files.

The term "delete" may be misleading, because files are not physically deleted from a disk file. DEL causes the file's entry on the disk directory to be flagged as deleted and the appropriate clusters in the FAT are shown as no longer being allocated.

Examples of usage:

`A> DEL B:MEMO.TXT` (deletes file MEMO.TXT from Drive B)

`A> DEL memo.*` (deletes all files from the Drive A named MEMO regardless of extension)

`B> del *.txt` (deletes all files on Drive B with a TXT extension)

TYPE Command

`TYPE [d:]filename[.ext]`

The **TYPE** command is used to display the contents of a "listable" file on the standard output device, normally the monitor. It does not alter files. This command should only be used for text files, but not for command files that end with an extension of .EXE or .COM. Wildcard characters are not allowed with the TYPE command.

Examples of usage:

`A> TYPE B:READ.ME` (displays on the screen the contents of READ.ME, stored on Drive B)

`A> type read.me` (displays on the screen the contents of READ.ME, stored on Drive A)

`A> TYPE AUTOEXEC.BAT >PRN` (types the contents of AUTOEXEC.BAT, redirecting the output from the screen to the printer. This is a handy technique for getting a hard copy listing of a file.)

SUMMARY OF NEW TERMS
Before data can be stored on a disk, the disk must be properly formatted to record files. The **FORMAT** command is used by DOS to establish acceptable clusters where data can be stored. In addition, it sets up a directory and File Allocation Table area on the disk to help DOS keep track of the files it saves. DOS tries to make it easier to enter commands by automatically converting all characters to upper case and by using the default disk concept. It assumes the files referred to in the commands are on the default disk unless you tell it otherwise. The full filename, used to identify files stored on disk, is made up of at least three parts: an optional disk-drive designator, a one- to eight-character filename, and an optional one- to three-character extension preceded by a period. The extension is useful in classifying the type of file on directory

listings. The **DIR** command is used to display a listing of files on a disk. By using wildcard characters with the DIR command, you can limit the listing to a specific group of files. The **DATE** and **TIME** commands are used to change the system date and time. The **DEL** command lets you delete files from a disk. The **TYPE** command lets you view the contents of text files.

Review Questions

1. What is a disk cluster?
2. What does the command DIR B:/P do when executed?
3. What is the purpose of the FORMAT command?
4. What is a filename extension? How is it identified by DOS?
5. What are some common extensions for listable files?
6. What are some common extensions for executable files?
7. Why might you want to use the /S option with FORMAT?
8. What is the benefit of using wildcard characters in the DIR command?
9. What command removes the filename from the disk directory, but does not actually erase the file from the disk?
10. What option allows you to get a directory listing on the screen with multiple filenames displayed on a line?
11. What command is used to get a directory listing of all files on Drive B with the extension .DOC?
12. What do you have to enter to change the system time to 4:00 P.M.?
13. What type of file is considered listable with TYPE?
14. What command covered in this chapter can be used to display the volume label on a disk?
15. How can you change the system date once the system is booted?
16. What special areas are created on a disk when it is formatted?
17. What is the structure of the full filename?
18. What part of the full filename is always required?
19. Explain the default disk drive concept.
20. At the B> system prompt, what command is entered to change the system prompt back to A>?

LAB EXERCISES – FLOPPY DISK USERS

1. After booting DOS, format a data disk to contain the DOS system files:

   - Enter FORMAT B:/S/V

   - When prompted, insert a blank disk in Drive B and press Enter.

   - Enter your name (up to eleven characters) when prompted to enter a volume label.

   - Enter N when prompted to format another disk.

   Figure 2-4 shows you what the screen should look like when you finish formatting your blank disk.

Figure 2-4

Screen Display of the FORMAT Command.

```
A>FORMAT B:/S/V

              FORMAT version 3.30.05
Copyright(C) 1988, Zenith Data Systems Corporation

Insert new disk in drive B:
and press RETURN when ready

Format complete
System transferred

Volume label (11 characters, RETURN for none)? DATA DISK


    362496 bytes total disk space
     81920 bytes used by system
    280576 bytes available on disk

Format another (Y/N)?N
A>
```

2. The COPY CON command, covered in the next chapter, can be used to quickly create a text file from the keyboard (CONsole):

   - Enter COPY CON B:READ.ME (or copy con b:read.me).

   - Then enter the following text exactly as shown, pressing the Enter key at the end of each line.

     When entering DOS commands, the commands and parameters must be separated by delimiters. Delimiters are normally either a space, a comma, or a semicolon. They can be used interchangeably within any command (i.e., COPY A:oldfile,B:).

DOS Essentials

- After entering the last line, press function key F6 (to tell DOS you are done with the copy operation) and press Enter. The text you just keyed is stored on the disk in Drive B with the filename of READ.ME.

  Figure 2-5 shows the screen after you have completed the COPY CON command.

Figure 2-5
Screen Display of COPY CON.

```
A>COPY CON B:READ.ME
When entering DOS commands, the commands and parameters
must be separated by delimiters.  Delimiters are normally
either a space, a comma, or a semicolon.  They can be used
interchangeably within any command (i.e., COPY A:oldfile,B:).
^Z
        1 File(s) copied

A>
```

3. Display a disk file on the monitor:
   - Enter DIR B: (to verify that your file was stored). This listing should include READ.ME plus the COMMAND.COM file placed there during formatting with the system option.
   - Enter TYPE B:READ.ME to display the contents of your text file on the monitor.

     Figure 2-6 shows you what the screen should look like when you finish this portion of the exercise.

Figure 2-6

*Screen Display of
DIR and TYPE.*

```
A>DIR B:

 Volume in drive B is DATA DISK
 Directory of  B:\

COMMAND  COM    25532  10-31-88   2:54p
READ     ME       239   9-23-90  11:37a
         2 File(s)    279552 bytes free

A>TYPE B:READ.ME
When entering DOS commands, the commands and parameters
must be separated by delimiters.  Delimiters are normally
either a space, a comma, or a semicolon.  They can be used
interchangeably within any command (i.e., COPY A:oldfile,B:).

A>
```

4. Delete a file from a disk:

   Before you experiment with the DEL command, the
   COPY command (Chapter 3) will be used to make an extra
   copy of an existing file.

   • Enter COPY B:READ.ME B:READ.BAK (to make a duplicate
     copy)
   • Enter DIR B: (to verify the file was copied)
   • Enter DEL B:READ.BAK
   • Enter DIR B: (to verify that the file was deleted)

   Your screen should look similar to that shown in Figure 2-7.

Figure 2-7

*Screen Display of
DEL and DIR*

```
A>DEL B:READ.BAK

A>DIR B:

 Volume in drive B is DATA DISK
 Directory of  B:\

COMMAND  COM    25532  10-31-88   2:54p
READ     ME       239   9-23-90  11:37a
         2 File(s)    279552 bytes free

A>
```

5. Change the default disk drive:

- Enter B: (to switch default to Drive B).
- Enter DIR (to get a directory of the default disk, Drive B).
- Enter DIR A:/W (to get a wide listing of Drive A).
- Enter A: (to change the default drive back to Drive A).

Don't be concerned if several lines have scrolled off the top of your screen. Your screen should look similar to Figure 2-8.

Figure 2-8
Screen Display of DIR.

```
A>B:

B>DIR

 Volume in drive B is DATA DISK
 Directory of  B:\

COMMAND  COM    25532  10-31-88   2:54p
READ     ME       239   9-23-90  11:37a
         2 File(s)    279552 bytes free

B>DIR A:/W

 Volume in drive A is DOS33
 Directory of  A:\

COMMAND  COM   ANSI     SYS    ATTRIB   EXE    BACKUP   COM    CHKDSK   COM
DISKCOPY COM   EDLIN    COM    FORMAT   COM    LABEL    COM    PARK     COM
RESTORE  COM   SORT     EXE    SYS      COM    TREE     COM    XCOPY    EXE
        15 File(s)    135168 bytes free

B>
```

6. Enter DATE and follow the prompts to change the current system date to December 25, 1991. Use the TIME command to change the system time to 1:45 P.M. Most users only enter hh:mm (i.e., 13:45) for the time and ignore entering seconds.

7. Bonus exercise:

- Use the DATE command to enter the current date. Then use the TIME command to make sure the system time is correct.
- Use the COPY CON command to create a new file called B:EX2.TXT. It should contain the following five lines of text, entered one line at a time, pressing the Enter key at the end of each line shown. After entering the last line of text, press the F6 key, then the Enter key.

The Lotus 1-2-3 software package, as the name implies, has three logical and integrated parts: spreadsheets, graphics, and data management. Integration means you do not have to leave the spreadsheet portion, for instance, to get to the graphing or data management portions.

- Use the TYPE command to display this newly created file.

- Using DOS wildcard characters, delete all files on Drive B with a filename of EX2 and any extension. Before you press the Enter key, be sure your command is keyed correctly, or you may delete more files than you intended. One file should be deleted. Display a directory listing to check the status of files on Drive B. It should look similar to Figure 2-7.

This completes the lab exercises for Chapter 2. Remember to remove your floppy disks before leaving the computer.

▌ LAB EXERCISES – HARD DISK USERS

1. After booting DOS, change to the directory containing your DOS commands (see instructor for specific instructions). Format a data disk to contain the DOS system files:

   - Enter FORMAT A:/S/V

   - When prompted, insert a blank disk in Drive A and press Enter.

   - Enter your name (up to eleven characters) when prompted to enter a volume label.

   - Enter N when prompted to format another disk.

   Figure 2-4 shows you what the screen should look similar to when you finish formatting your blank disk.

2. The COPY CON command, covered in the next chapter, can be used to quickly create a text file from the keyboard (CONsole):

   - Enter COPY CON A:READ.ME (or copy con a:read.me).

   - Then enter the following text exactly as shown, pressing the Enter key at the end of each line.

     When entering DOS commands, the commands and parameters must be separated by delimiters. Delimiters are normally either a space, a comma, or a semicolon. They can be used interchangeably within any command (i.e., COPY A:oldfile,B:).

- After entering the last line, press function key F6 (to tell DOS you are done with the copy operation) and press Enter. The text you just keyed is stored on the disk in Drive A with the filename of READ.ME.

  Figure 2-5 shows the screen after you have completed the COPY CON command.

3. Display a disk file on the monitor:
   - Enter DIR A: (to verify that your file was stored). This listing should include READ.ME plus the COMMAND.COM file placed there during formatting with the system option.
   - Enter TYPE A:READ.ME to display the contents of your text file on the monitor.

     Figure 2-6 shows you what the screen should look similar to when you finish this portion of the exercise.

4. Delete a file from a disk:
   Before you experiment with the DEL command, the COPY command (Chapter 3) will be used to make an extra copy of an existing file.
   - Enter COPY A:READ.ME A:READ.BAK (to make a duplicate copy)
   - Enter DIR A: (to verify the file was copied)
   - Enter DEL A:READ.BAK
   - Enter DIR A: (to verify that the file was deleted)

     Your screen should look similar to that shown in Figure 2-7.

5. Change the default disk drive:
   - Enter A: (to switch default to Drive A).
   - Enter DIR (to get a directory of the default disk, Drive A).
   - Enter DIR C:/W (to get a wide listing of Drive C).
   - Enter C: (to change the default drive back to Drive C).

     Don't be concerned if several lines have scrolled off the top of your screen. Your screen should look similar to Figure 2-8.

6. Enter DATE and follow the prompts to change the current system date to December 25, 1991. Use the TIME command to change the system time to 1:45 P.M. Most users only enter hh:mm (i.e., 13:45) for the time and ignore entering seconds.

7. Bonus exercise:

   • Use the DATE command to enter the current date. Then use the TIME command to make sure the system time is correct.

   • Use the COPY CON command to create a new file called A:EX2.TXT. It should contain the following five lines of text, entered one line at a time, pressing the Enter key at the end of each line shown. After entering the last line of text, press the F6 key, then the Enter key.

   The Lotus 1-2-3 software package, as the name implies, has three logical and integrated parts: spreadsheets, graphics, and data management. Integration means you do not have to leave the spreadsheet portion, for instance, to get to the graphing or data management portions.

   • Use the TYPE command to display this newly created file.

   • Using DOS wildcard characters, delete all files on Drive A with a filename of EX2 and any extension. Before you press the Enter key, be sure your command is keyed correctly, or you may delete more files than you intended. One file should be deleted. Display a directory listing to check the status of files on Drive A. It should look similar to Figure 2-7.

   This completes the lab exercises for Chapter 2. Remember to remove your floppy disk before leaving the computer.

Additional DOS Commands

There are three major objectives of Chapter 3: First is to review the most common error messages so you'll know what to do if one occurs. Second is to show how DISKCOPY and COPY can be used to make backup copies of important files. The last objective is to show how to use three more essential commands: CHKDSK, RENAME, and VER.

COMMON DOS ERROR MESSAGES
Commands you enter may be rejected by DOS, resulting in the error message **"Bad Command or Filename."** This message can occur when the command was not spelled correctly, DOS cannot find the command, or a filename was not on the specified disk. If this error message appears, simply retype the command correctly. If you attempt to read a disk while either no disk is in the designated drive or the drive latch is open, you get the following two-line error message, where X is the disk drive with the error:

```
Disk error reading Drive X
Abort, Retry, Ignore?
```

If you get this message, correct the problem and enter R to retry. You can also enter A to abort the command or I to ignore the error condition. It is not advisable to ignore error messages (I), however, nor should you change disks before responding with R.

The space between the read/write heads and the surface of the disks is incredibly small. Therefore, any movement of the disk drive when the disk is operating can be very destructive.

When you attempt to access damaged data or read an unformatted disk, you see the following message displayed:

```
General Failure reading Drive X
Abort, Retry, or Ignore?
```

THE IMPORTANCE OF BACKUP

All disks may be subject to damage from time to time. Files on floppy disks can become unreadable because of fingerprints, dirt, and improperly adjusted read/write heads. Hard disk drives can be severely damaged if they are moved without the read/write heads parked correctly. And static electricity can disrupt the data magnetically recorded on all disks. Therefore, you should periodically **back up** important files, especially if they are difficult to re-create. Individual files can easily be backed up using the COPY command. The DISKCOPY command is generally used to back up an entire disk.

DISKCOPY Command

```
[d:]DISKCOPY [d:[d:]]
```

DISKCOPY is an external command that resides on the DOS disk. It is used to copy the entire contents of one floppy disk to another floppy disk. It copies the directory portion of the disk, the File Allocation Table, and all files. Because DISKCOPY makes an exact duplicate of the source disk, it does not require the target disk be formatted. It cannot be used to duplicate a hard disk. Nor can it be used to copy floppy disks that are physically different (i.e., a 360KB 5¼″ disk and a 1.44MB 3½″ disk).

Two problems can occur when using DISKCOPY. By attempting to make a duplicate copy of the source disk, it is possible for data from good clusters to be copied into corresponding clusters on the target disk that are damaged. Data written in bad clusters cannot be retrieved by DOS.

The second limitation of using DISKCOPY is that fragmented files on the source disk are written in the same fragmented clusters on the target disk. The COPY command, covered next, eliminates both of the problems inherent with DISKCOPY.

Examples of usage:

A> DISKCOPY A: B: (makes an exact copy of the disk in Drive A onto a disk in Drive B)

`A> diskcopy a:` (makes a copy of the first disk inserted into Drive A onto a second disk inserted into Drive A when prompted)

COPY Command

`COPY [d:]filename[.ext] [d:][filename[.ext]]`

> where the first filename is the source file and the second filename (optional) is the target file (the new file being created).

The **COPY** command lets you make copies of disk files to a previously formatted disk. It facilitates making backup or working copies of files without destroying existing files. However, any files on the target disk with the same name as the target file are replaced by the contents of the source file by the copy operation.

If you omit a disk device designator [d:], DOS substitutes the default device. If you omit the optional target filename, the system uses the same filename as the source file.

You can copy a group of files with a single command by using wildcard characters in filenames with the COPY command. For example, to copy all files on Drive A with an extension of DOC to Drive B, enter:

`COPY A:*.DOC B:`

If you specify the source file as CON (used by DOS to identify the CONsole keyboard), the target file contains characters you enter from the keyboard. Type characters as you would from a typewriter, pressing the Enter key at the end of each line. Lines are limited to 127 characters each. DOS uses Ctrl-Z to mark the end of a text file. To stop recording characters and to insert the Ctrl-Z character, press the F6 function key, <F6>, followed by the Enter key. For example:

`COPY CON A:KBFILE.TXT` (followed by lines of text and <F6>)

Examples of usage:

`A> COPY *.* B:` (copies all files on the default disk, Drive A, to the disk in Drive B, without renaming files)

`A> copy B:*.DOC` (copies all files on Drive B with an extension of DOC to the default disk)

`A> Copy filea.doc b:filea.bak` (copies FILEA.DOC on Drive A to Drive B, renaming it FILEA.BAK)

`A> copy con b:read.me` (creates a file on Drive B named READ.ME consisting of lines of data entered from console)

A> COPY A:*.DOC B:*.BAK (copies all files on Drive A with a DOC extension to Drive B, renaming them with an extension of BAK)

A> COPY FILEA.DOC PRN (copies a text file to the printer)

MORE ESSENTIAL DOS COMMANDS

CHKDSK Command

[d:]CHKDSK [d:][filename[.ext]] [/V]

CHKDSK (Check Disk) is an external command (CHKDSK.COM) stored on the DOS disk. It produces a disk status report for a specified disk and lists the memory status of the system. After checking the disk, CHKDSK displays any error messages, followed by a status report. The following is an example of a CHKDSK status report, where the drive designated was a floppy disk and there were no errors detected:

Volume DATADISK   Created JUL 15, 1991 11:35a

362496 bytes total disk space
  23528 bytes in 3 hidden files
311296 bytes in 29 user files
  27672 bytes available on disk

655360 bytes total memory
568112 bytes free

The three hidden files in the status report represent the volume label and two DOS system files. Remember, hidden files do not show as entries on a directory listing. The bottom portion of the report represents the memory status of a computer with 640KB of RAM. The difference between the 655,360 bytes of total memory shown above and the 568,112 bytes free is about 85KB. That is the amount of RAM space allocated to the RAM-resident portion of DOS and the space required to load CHKDSK.COM.

New files are written to contiguous clusters whenever the first unallocated space found is big enough. The recording of an existing file that has been enlarged can cause problems, however. When the original file space has been rewritten, DOS continues writing to the next unallocated cluster on the disk. It writes in consecutive clusters, skipping over those that are already allocated. Consequently, files can easily become fragmented as they expand over time.

Perhaps the most common use of CHKDSK is to identify what files on a disk are fragmented. If you specify a filename, CHKDSK displays the number of noncontiguous areas occupied by the file. Wildcard characters can be used for the filename. Thus, you can use *.* to determine the extent of file fragmentation on a disk and then use the COPY command to rewrite fragmented files to a newly formatted disk. This process is recommended to improve access speed.

The /V option (Visual) allows you to display all files and their complete pathname (Chapter 4) on a specified drive. This option can be beneficial with hard disk systems.

Examples of usage:

A> CHKDSK (display a status report for the default drive)

A> chkdsk B:read.me (display a status report for Drive B and display the number of noncontiguous areas contained in READ.ME)

B> CHKDSK /V (displays a status report of Drive B and lists all files on Drive B, displaying their full filenames)

B> a:chkdsk *.* (display a status report for Drive B, identifying any fragmented files — CHKDSK.COM is stored on Drive A)

RENAME Command

RENAME [d:]filename[.ext] filename[.ext]

The **RENAME** command changes the name of the file specified in the first parameter to the filename given in the second parameter. A drive designator is not allowed in the second parameter and is rejected if entered. RENAME gives you an easy way to make disguised copies of important files. For example, a spreadsheet file called BUDGET.WK1 could be renamed WORK.EXE. A shortened and commonly used version of the RENAME command is REN.

Examples of usage:

A> RENAME b:ltr1.doc ltr1.bak (renames ltr1.doc on Drive B to ltr1.bak)

A> ren Ltr1.doc ltr1.bak (renames ltr1.doc on Drive A to ltr1.bak)

A> REN *.TXT *.DOC (renames all files with a .TXT extension to an extension of .DOC)

A> ren ltr1.doc *.bak (renames ltr1.doc on Drive A to ltr1.bak — use of wildcard characters can save keystrokes)

VER (Version) Command

VER

    The **VER** command displays the DOS version number being used on the screen (i.e., IBM Personal Computer DOS Version 3.10). If you boot your system with one version of DOS, then attempt to execute external DOS commands from a disk with a different version, you may get an "Incorrect DOS Version" error message. The VER command is used to identify the DOS version used to boot your system.

SUMMARY OF NEW TERMS

It is not uncommon for users to have error messages flashed on the screen when using DOS. The most common message is "Bad Command or Filename." This simply means that DOS cannot recognize the command entered, or it cannot find a file specified in the command. It is also possible for files on disks to become damaged (unreadable). Therefore, it is recommended that backup copies (duplicates) be made of important files from time to time. The **DISKCOPY** command can be used to make copies of all files on one disk to another disk. To avoid problems associated with DISKCOPY, you can use the COPY command. The **COPY** command is also used to copy selected files from one disk to another, or to make a duplicate copy on the same disk, using a different filename. If you experience problems with a disk, the **CHKDSK** command can be used to determine the extent of file fragmentation and report on the overall status of file space. The **RENAME** command is used to give files a new name, without having to copy the file. The **VER** command is used to quickly identify the version of DOS in use.

Review Questions

1. What is the function of brackets in this text for describing command formats?

2. What is the function of the slash in this text for describing command formats?

3. What is a delimiter? Why is it required?

4. What does the message "Bad Command or File Name" mean?

5. Where are internal commands stored on a permanent basis?

6. Why is it important to back up files occasionally?

7. What does the COPY CON command let you do?

8. What happens when you enter the following command:

   `A>COPY TEST.TXT B:`

9. What is the benefit of using wildcard characters in the COPY command?

10. What happens when you enter this command?

    `A>COPY *.TXT B:*.BAK`

11. What happens if you include a disk drive designator on both parameters of the RENAME command?

12. What command is used to verify the DOS version being used?

13. Where do external commands reside when not executing?

14. What are two types of hidden files on a system disk?

15. What are fragmented disk files?

16. How can you determine the amount of file fragmentation on a disk?

17. How can you improve access speeds of disks that contain fragmented files?

18. What is the primary difference between using the COPY command rather than using the DISKCOPY command?

19. Which DOS command lists all files on a disk and displays their full filenames?

20. Under what circumstance can you get the message "Incorrect DOS Version"?

LAB EXERCISES – FLOPPY DISK USERS

1. Boot DOS (Drive A), and insert your data disk in Drive B. Then enter DIR B: to refresh your memory of the files on Drive B. You should see two files displayed, which were previously created in Chapter 2 Lab Exercises: COMMAND.COM and READ.ME.

2. Enter COPY B:READ.ME B:READ.BAK to create a duplicate copy of READ.ME with a different extension. What would happen if you entered the command without the last parameter (B:READ.BAK)? DOS would have substituted the default disk and used the source filename, creating the backup copy on Drive A with the same name.

3. Enter DIR B: to get a current directory listing of your data disk. Enter RENAME B:READ.BAK TEST.TXT to change the filename of READ.BAK on your data disk. Enter DIR B: to verify the name change. Your screen should look similar to Figure 3-1.

Figure 3-1
Screen Display of DIR.

```
A>DIR B:

 Volume in drive B is DATA DISK
 Directory of  B:\

COMMAND  COM   25532  10-31-88   2:54p
READ     ME      239   9-23-90  11:37a
READ     BAK     239   9-23-90  11:37a
        3 File(s)    278528 bytes free

A>REN B:READ.BAK TEST.TXT

A>DIR B:

 Volume in drive B is DATA DISK
 Directory of  B:\

COMMAND  COM   25532  10-31-88   2:54p
READ     ME      239   9-23-90  11:37a
TEST     TXT     239   9-23-90  11:37a
        3 File(s)    278528 bytes free

A>
```

4. Enter VER to see which DOS version you are using.

5. Enter CHKDSK to get a status report of the default drive (A:). Now enter CHKDSK B:*.* to get a status report of your data disk, directing the system to check for any fragmented files. Figure 3-2 shows you the display screen after running CHKDSK. Your display screen should look similar to this one.

Figure 3-2

Screen Display of CHKDSK.

```
A>CHKDSK
Volume DOS33        created Jan 28, 1990 6:46a

    362496 bytes total disk space
     56320 bytes in 3 hidden files
    171008 bytes in 15 user files
    135168 bytes available on disk

    655360 bytes total memory
    588752 bytes free

A>CHKDSK B:*.*
Volume DATA DISK    created Sep 23, 1990 11:36a

    362496 bytes total disk space
     56320 bytes in 3 hidden files
     27648 bytes in 3 user files
    278528 bytes available on disk

    655360 bytes total memory
    588752 bytes free

All specified file(s) are contiguous.

A>
```

6. Use CHKDSK with the /V option to get a listing of all the files on your DOS disk. Then use it to view the files on your data disk.

7. Bonus exercise:

- Using the RENAME command, change all files on Drive B with a filename of TEST (and any extension) to NEWNAME. Use wildcard characters whenever possible. Use the DIR command to confirm the results.

- Now, copy all files on Drive B with a filename of NEWNAME to a filename of TEST, without changing the filename extension. Display all the files on Drive B to confirm the operation was successful. Finally, delete all files on Drive B with a filename of NEWNAME.

   This completes Chapter 3 lab exercises. When you are done, be sure to remove your disks.

LAB EXERCISES – HARD DISK USERS

1. Boot DOS (Drive C), insert your data disk in Drive A, and change to the directory containing the DOS commands. Then enter DIR A: to refresh your memory of the files on Drive A. You should see two files displayed, which were previously created in Chapter 2 Lab Exercises: COMMAND.COM and READ.ME.

2. Enter COPY A:READ.ME A:READ.BAK to create a duplicate copy of READ.ME with a different extension. What would happen if you entered the command without the last parameter (A:READ.BAK)? DOS would have substituted the default disk and used the source filename, creating the backup copy on Drive C with the same name.

3. Enter DIR A: to get a current directory listing of your data disk. Enter RENAME A:READ.BAK TEST.TXT to change the filename of READ.BAK on your data disk. Enter DIR A: to verify the name change. Your screen should look similar to Figure 3-1.

4. Enter VER to see which DOS version you are using.

5. Enter CHKDSK to get a status report of the default drive (C:). Now enter CHKDSK A:*.* to get a status report of your data disk, directing the system to check for any fragmented files. Figure 3-2 shows you the display screen after running CHKDSK. Your display screen should look similar to this one.

6. Use CHKDSK with the /V option to get a listing of all the files on your DOS disk. Then use it to view the files on your data disk.

7. Bonus exercise:
   - Using the RENAME command, change all files on Drive A with a filename of TEST (and any extension) to NEWNAME. Use wildcard characters whenever possible. Use the DIR command to confirm the results.
   - Now, copy all files on Drive A with a filename of NEWNAME to a filename of TEST, without changing the filename extension. Display all the files on Drive A to confirm the operation was successful. Finally, delete all files on Drive A with a filename of NEWNAME.

   This completes Chapter 3 lab exercises. When you are done, be sure to remove your disks.

Hard Disk Commands

The major objective of Chapter 4 is to show you how to work with hard disks and subdirectories. This includes five essential hard disk commands: MD, CD, RD, PATH, and PROMPT.

HARD DISK CONSIDERATIONS When you first
use a **hard disk system**, you should notice two significant improvements over processing with floppy disks. First, the speed at which data can be transferred with hard disks is 10-20 times faster than with floppy disks. The second improvement is the amount of data that can be stored on hard disks. A 20MB hard disk can hold the equivalent of fifty-five floppy disks.

The use of hard disks creates some considerations that are not as relevant when using floppy disks. The first consideration is the need for a good power supply that does not permit loss of electrical power. A temporary power loss can cause the disk's read/write heads to "crash" on the surface of the disk, causing permanent damage.

A second consideration is the need to periodically back up the data stored on your hard disk to floppy disks. Hard disk users tend to overlook this process but you should get into the habit of backing up your hard disks regularly. You will be glad you did the day you turn on your computer and hear a noise like a spoon in a blender.

Another consideration is the need to move the read/write heads to an unused area of the hard disk before you "power down" the system. When the power is turned off, the read/write heads on some hard disk drives do not retract automatically. Instead, they settle down on the surface of the hard disk. Over time, this process can damage data stored on the disk. Because not all hard disks automatically retract the heads, you should execute a program like PARK or SHIPDISK that moves the heads to a vacant cylinder just prior to turning off the power.

DIRECTORIES AND SUBDIRECTORIES Because

large amounts of data can be stored on a hard disk, it is extremely helpful to divide the total space into uniquely named areas. Each area can be reserved to store a group of files, allowing you to organize and classify files by area. DOS uses a **root directory** and optional **subdirectories** (directories within a directory) to keep track of the name and location of all files on disk. The term directory is often used in place of subdirectory. You can establish directories for floppy disks, but the use of directories is more practical for hard disks.

One way to visualize the concept of directories is to compare a single 20MB hard disk to a set of fifty-five floppy disks. Conceptually, each directory could represent a single floppy disk, without the capacity limitations of a single floppy disk, however. And, like floppy disks, each directory could be devoted to a given application, such as word processing, spreadsheets, accounting, and so on. Just as you change floppy disks, you can also change to another directory. Additionally, just as such commands as DEL, DIR, and COPY relate to a given floppy disk, they apply to a given directory.

You can organize and control hundreds of files on hard disk by adopting a tree-structured file directory system. The root directory branches into directories. The directories, in turn, can branch into further directories in a hierarchy much like that of a family tree. Each directory is assigned a unique name using the same rules we use with filenames. Floppy disk files are often organized manually by recording selected groups of files on a disk and identifying each disk with a label. Directories provide a big advantage in that they let you organize files on a hard disk electronically. Within each directory, files can be added and new directories can be created. Figure 4-1 shows a graphic example of a tree-structured directory.

Figure 4-1

Sample Hierarchy of Subdirectories.

```
                              ┌─────────────┐
                              │  C:\ (root)  │
                              └──────┬──────┘
                   ┌─────────────────┴─────────────────┐
            ┌──────────┐                        ┌───────────┐
            │  C:\Word │                        │  C:\Lotus │
            └────┬─────┘                        └─────┬─────┘
       ┌─────────┼─────────┐                ┌─────────┴─────────┐
 ┌──────────┐┌──────────┐┌──────────┐ ┌──────────┐      ┌──────────┐
 │C:\Word\Book││C:\Word\Memo││C:\Word\Ltrs│ │C:\Lotus\Curr│   │C:\Lotus\Hist│
 └──────────┘└──────────┘└──────────┘ └──────────┘      └──────────┘
```

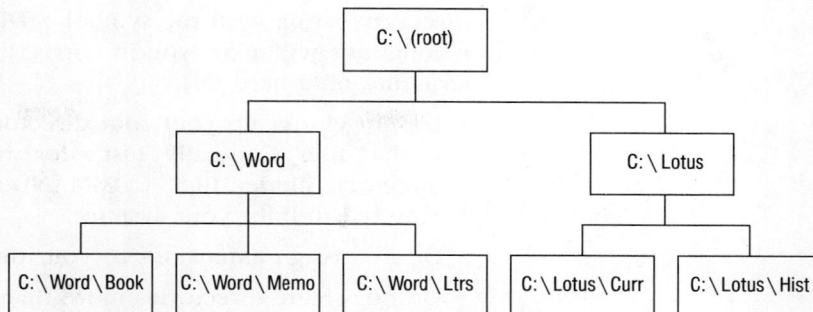

In this sample tree structure, the root directory is divided into two directories: one for word processing and one for spreadsheets. The word-processing directory, WORD, is further subdivided into three directories: one for a manuscript, one for memos, and one for letters. You can navigate through this structure by starting at the root and traveling down any of the desired branches to get to the desired directory.

DOS uses the backslash (\) to identify a directory name. Thus, the file BOSS.DOC stored on the MEMO directory is identified with the full name C:\WORD\MEMO\BOSS.DOC. The full filename identifies a path of directories that must be taken by DOS to find the file in the hierarchy. If the path is not included in the filename, the system looks for the file on the current directory. The backslash at the beginning of the path directs DOS to begin the path with the root directory. If the \ is not included, the path begins with the current directory. If the file you need is not on the current directory, you must provide DOS the path to find it. This path must be part of the full filename, just as the disk designator is supplied when a file is not on the default drive.

It is advantageous to set up directories so that program files are separated from data files. This way, users can easily back up the directories containing data files without having to back up the unchanged program files. Directories containing program files only need to be backed up once, unless new programs are added.

DOS has several commands that allow you to create and use directories. Any reference to the ''current directory'' refers to the directory you are currently working in. You can change to another directory at any time. Entries on a directory include filenames and directory names. Directories are identified on a directory listing with the symbol <DIR>. The following recommendations will assist you in correctly setting up the directory structure on a hard disk:

- Do not clutter up your root directory with too many programs or data files. Generally, just a few files need to be in the root directory: hidden files, COMMAND.COM, and any other files required to boot your system.
- Do not assign extensions to your directory names.
- Do not create directories more than two or three levels below the root directory.
- Give your directories short but meaningful names, such as: \DOS, \UTIL, \WORD, \DB, \SS, and so on.
- Do not give a file the same name as its directory name.

DOS COMMANDS RELATED TO DIRECTORIES
Figure 4-2 lists five essential commands used with hard disk systems. They are all internal DOS commands.

Figure 4-2
Hard Disk Command Summary.

```
MD – Make Directory (creates a directory)
CD – Change Directory (changes to an existing directory)
RD – Remove Directory (eliminates a directory)
PATH – Instructs DOS where to look for command files
PROMPT – Changes the system prompt
```

MD (Make Directory) Command

```
MD [d:]path
```

The **MD** command creates a new directory on the disk. You may create as many directories as you want, but too many can cause confusion. Each directory can contain both filenames and directory names that occur on other directories, but all directory names as well as all filenames must be unique within a directory.

Example of usage:

C> MD \word (creates a directory named WORD one level down from the root directory, assuming it does not already exist in the root directory)

C> md \word\MEMO (creates the directory MEMO one level down from the directory named WORD)

C> Md games (creates a directory called GAMES one level down from the current directory)

CD (Change Directory) Command

CD [d:][path]

The **CD** command changes from the current directory to another directory. The path is used to identify the new directory. For example, if you want to change to the root directory, enter CD\. A leading backslash (\) in the path directs DOS to start the path at the root directory. Normally, you want to start the path name at the root directory to make sure DOS is able to find it. You can enter the CD command with no parameters to display the current directory.

In directory listings you see "dot" and "double-dot" directory entries, like this:

.	<DIR>	8-15-91	9:45a
..	<DIR>	8-15-91	9:45a

These entries are automatically created by DOS to help it keep track of the directory tree structure. The dot entry represents the current directory and the double-dot entry represents the parent directory, one level up from the current directory. The double-dot entry can be used to quickly change to the parent directory. For example, the command "CD .." entered from the LOTUS\CURR directory, changes to the LOTUS directory.

You can save keystrokes by recognizing that the symbols \ and .. are considered delimiters in DOS commands, just like a space and the slash (/). Thus, the command "CD\" is interpreted the same as "CD \". The command "CD.." is the same as "CD ..".

Examples of usage:

C> CD \ (change to the root directory)

C> Cd (display the current directory)

`C> cd\word\memo` (change to the directory named MEMO on the WORD directory, starting from the root directory)

`C> CD WORD\MEMO` (change to the directory identified as MEMO on the WORD directory, starting from the current directory)

RD (Remove Directory) Command

`RD [d:]path`

The **RD** command removes a directory from disk. Before you can remove a directory, all files in that directory must be deleted and any subdirectories must be removed. To remove the current directory, you must first change to another directory before attempting to remove it. You cannot remove the root directory.

Examples of usage:

`C> rd \word\memo` (remove the directory named MEMO from the WORD directory)

`C> RD\WORD` (remove directory WORD from the root directory)

`C> rd memo` (remove directory MEMO from the current directory)

PATH Command

`PATH [d:][path][;path][;path]`

The command you want to execute may not always be on the current directory. The **PATH** command provides DOS the names of directories to search to find a command whenever DOS cannot find it on the current directory. The types of commands it can search for include the DOS external commands and application programs, such as WP, LOTUS, or dBASE.

Issuing a PATH command does not change the current directory. PATH only locates files that can be executed, such as files that have an extension of .COM or .EXE. Typing PATH with no parameters displays the current path. Entering PATH with just a semicolon tells the system you do not want any search path.

Examples of usage:

C> Path \DOS3 (directs the system to look on the directory named DOS3, whenever DOS cannot find the desired command on the current directory)

C> PATH\word\ltrs (directs the system to look on LTRS within WORD to find the external command it is looking for, if it is not on the current directory)

C> path (displays the current search path setting)

C> Path ; (deletes any previous search path setting)

C> PATH \;\UTIL;\DOS (directs DOS to search three directories in the order given: root, \UTIL, and \DOS)

PROMPT Command

PROMPT [text], where text is a variable-length string of characters. Text may contain special strings in the form of $c, where c represents one of the following:

t — system time
d — system date
n — default (current) drive
g — the > character
p — current directory

The **PROMPT** command lets you change the system prompt from the default (A>) to whatever you want to make it. If you enter PROMPT with no text, the system reverts back to the default prompt. When using hard disk systems, it is very helpful to replace the default system prompt with one that displays the current directory. This is normally accomplished with the command PROMPT PG. Figure 4-3 shows the effect on the screen of executing the four other examples of the PROMPT command shown below.

Examples of Usage:

A> PROMPT Command? (changes the system prompt from A> to Command?)

A> prompt DATE = $D (changes the system prompt to display DATE = followed by the system date)

A> prompt Hi Fred ng (displays Hi Fred followed by A>)

A> PROMPT (returns to the default system prompt)

Figure 4-3
*Screen Display of
PROMPT.*

```
A>PROMPT Command?

Command?prompt DATE = $D

DATE = Sun  9-23-1990prompt Hi Fred $n$g

Hi Fred A>PROMPT

A>
```

USEFUL HARD DISK-RELATED FILES

There are two special files that can be used by DOS to modify the way it runs: the **CONFIG.SYS** file and the **AUTOEXEC.BAT** file. When DOS is booted, the system automatically looks for these files on the root directory of the disk used to boot DOS.

CONFIG.SYS File

Immediately after the COMMAND.COM file and two hidden system files are loaded into RAM, DOS looks for the CONFIG.SYS file. The entries in this file let you specify how your system should operate and be configured. Typically, CONFIG.SYS lets you control the way memory is used and install device driver programs for controlling other devices. It is a text file of special DOS configuration commands that can be created with the COPY CON command. Here are the two CONFIG.SYS file entries most often used:

BUFFERS = nn
FILES = nn

In the BUFFERS entry, nn is the number of input/output buffers needed to improve disk performance. By specifying a relatively high number of buffers, you allow DOS to read a larger than usual chunk of data from your disk at one time. Then, whenever your program needs data, DOS checks to see if it is already in the RAM buffer. If it is, access is almost immediate. A recommended setting of fifteen to twenty buffers will suit most circumstances.

In the FILES entry, nn is the number of files that can be used at any one time by your programs. Because database applications often require twenty files open at the same time, the recommended number of open files is twenty to twenty-five.

AUTOEXEC.BAT File

The last step in the boot process is to execute an optional AUTOEXEC.BAT file. This batch file can simplify the boot process by executing a desired set of commands automatically. Batch files are covered in Chapter 5. Figure 4-4 shows you what the contents of a typical AUTOEXEC.BAT file might look like. It prompts the user to enter the correct system date and time, changes the system prompt, defines the search path for DOS, then executes an application program named PAYROLL.EXE.

Figure 4-4
Sample AUTOEXEC.BAT File.

```
DATE
TIME
PROMPT $P$G
PATH C:\DOS;C:\UTIL;C:\WORD
PAYROLL
```

SUMMARY OF NEW TERMS
Hard disk systems are significantly different from floppy disk systems. Not only are they much faster than floppy disks, but they can store much more data than a single floppy disk. Floppy disks are normally used to store duplicate backup copies of important hard disk files. Because so many files can be stored on a single hard disk, it is divided into subdirectories. The term directory is often used to refer to a subdirectory. The backslash (\) identifies a directory name. DOS commands let you make a directory (**MD**), a change to a directory (**CD**), and remove a directory (**RD**). Just like DOS needs to know which floppy disk to find a file, it needs to know the directory (path) to locate a hard disk file. If the path is not included in a command, a default path is used. The **PATH** command is used to define the default path. The **PROMPT** command can be used to display the current directory name as part of the DOS system prompt. A special file (CONFIG.SYS) can be used to improve the way files are processed in RAM. When DOS is booted, entries on the CONFIG.SYS file are used to configure (modify) the system. The last step in the boot process involves another optional file. Commands in an AUTOEXEC.BAT file are automatically executed by DOS.

Review Questions

1. How are files arranged or organized on hard disks?

2. Why is a constant supply of good electrical power especially important when using hard disks?

3. What is the purpose of the PARK or SHIPDISK commands?

4. What advantages do hard disks have over using floppy disks?

5. How are subdirectories designated in DOS?

6. What is a DOS path?

7. Why might you want to have relatively short directory names?

8. What command allows you to switch from the current directory to another directory?

9. How do you switch to the root directory?

10. How can identical filenames (i.e., FORMAT.COM) exist multiple times on the same hard disk?

11. If the current directory is C:\WORD\MEMO (See Figure 4-1), what command is entered to create a directory named DOS as a part of the root directory?

12. If the current directory is C:\WORD\MEMO (See Figure 4-1), what command is entered to create a directory named BOSS as a part of the current directory?

13. What is necessary to be able to remove a directory from a disk?

14. If multiple directories are included in a search path, which one is searched first?

15. How are multiple directories specified in the PATH command?

16. What command is used to view the current search path?

17. What command is used to change the system prompt to display the system time?

18. What is the DOS command to a customized system prompt displaying the system date, system time, and the correct directory followed by the ">"?

19. Why is it beneficial to have program files in separate directories from data files?

20. What is the double-dot (..) entry on a directory listing?

LAB EXERCISES – FLOPPY DISK USERS

To keep from interfering with an existing hard disk structure, directories are created and used on a floppy disk.

1. Make a hierarchy of directories on Drive B according to Figure 4-1 of this text as follows:

   A> MD B:\WORD

   A> MD B:\WORD\BOOK

   A> MD B:\WORD\MEMO

   A> MD B:\WORD\LTRS

   A> MD B:\LOTUS

   A> MD B:\LOTUS\CURR

   A> MD B:\LOTUS\HIST

2. Copy one of the files currently residing on the root directory of Drive B to each of the seven directories created above. For Example: COPY B:READ.ME B:\WORD

3. Check out your new directory structure by entering:

   C> DIR B: (lists files and directories in root directory)

   C> DIR B:\WORD (lists all files and directories in \WORD — the screen should look similar to Figure 4-5)

Figure 4-5

Screen Display of Directories on \WORD

```
A>DIR B:

Volume in drive B is DATA DISK
Directory of  B:\

COMMAND  COM    25532  10-31-88   2:54p
READ     ME       239   9-23-90  11:37a
TEST     TXT      239   9-23-90  11:37a
WORD          <DIR>      9-23-90  11:56a
LOTUS         <DIR>      9-23-90  11:57a
        5 File(s)    264192 bytes free

A>DIR B:\WORD

 Volume in drive B is DATA DISK
 Directory of  B:\WORD

              <DIR>      9-23-90  11:56a
.             <DIR>      9-23-90  11:56a
BOOK          <DIR>      9-23-90  11:57a
MEMO          <DIR>      9-23-90  11:57a
LTRS          <DIR>      9-23-90  11:57a
READ     ME      239   9-23-90  11:37a
        6 File(s)    264192 bytes free

A>
```

4. Make the current directory MEMO:

   A> B: (change default drive to B to minimize keystrokes)

   B> CD\WORD\MEMO (make MEMO the current directory)

   B> DIR (test change to desired directory only)

   B> CD\ (change back to root directory)

   B> DIR (list all files and directories on the root directory)

5. While still using Drive B as the default drive, delete the directory named HIST:

   B> DEL \LOTUS\HIST*.* (delete all files from HIST first)

   B> RD \LOTUS\HIST (remove HIST directory)

6. Set up a path to your DOS external commands:

   B> PATH A: (set path to include Drive A)

   B> CHKDSK (test the path noting that DOS finds CHKDSK on Drive A *after* first searching Drive B, the default drive.)

7. Change the system prompt to display a message with the system date. Enter the following:

   PROMPT It is dg What is your command?

   Execute a few commands (such as DIR, VOL, and VER) to experience the new system prompt. Then return the system prompt back to its default by entering PROMPT NG.

8. Change the system prompt to display the current directory. Then change to several directories to see the effect:

   B> PROMPT PG

   B> CD\WORD

   B> CD\LOTUS\CURR

   B> CD\

9. Bonus Exercise:

   • Change the default disk to Drive B. Copy at least two files from the root directory of Drive B to the WORD directory created above.

   • Create a directory (TEMP) from the root directory of Drive B.

- Change to TEMP, copy all files from B:\WORD to TEMP, and use the DIR command to verify the copy process. Use wildcard characters whenever possible to save keystrokes and minimize errors.

- Finally, remove the TEMP directory and change back to the A> prompt. Did you remember to delete the files in TEMP first?

This ends Chapter 4 lab exercises. Remove your disks when you are done, and remember, "practice is the best teacher."

LAB EXERCISES – HARD DISK USERS

To keep from interfering with an existing hard disk structure, directories are created and used on a floppy disk.

1. Make a hierarchy of directories on Drive A according to Figure 4-1 of this text as follows:

   `C> MD A:\WORD`

   `C> MD A:\WORD\BOOK`

   `C> MD A:\WORD\MEMO`

   `C> MD A:\WORD\LTRS`

   `C> MD A:\LOTUS`

   `C> MD A:\LOTUS\CURR`

   `C> MD A:\LOTUS\HIST`

2. Copy one of the files currently residing on the root directory of Drive A to each of the seven directories created above. For Example: COPY A:READ.ME A:\WORD

3. Check out your new directory structure by entering:

   `C> DIR A:` (lists files and directories in root directory)

   `C> DIR A:\WORD` (lists all files and directories in \WORD — the screen should look similar to Figure 4-5)

4. Make the current directory MEMO:

   `C> A:` (change default drive to A to minimize keystrokes)

   `A> CD\WORD\MEMO` (make MEMO the current directory)

   `A> DIR` (test change to desired directory only)

   `A> CD\` (change back to root directory)

   `A> DIR` (list all files and directories on the root directory)

5. While still using Drive A as the default drive, delete the directory named HIST:

   `A> DEL \LOTUS\HIST\*.*` (delete all files from HIST first)

   `A> RD \LOTUS\HIST` (remove HIST directory)

6. Because your hard disk system may already have an active path, check with your instructor before doing this exercise. Set up a path to your DOS external commands:

   `A> PATH C:` (set path to include Drive C)

   `A> CHKDSK` (test the path noting that DOS finds CHKDSK on Drive C *after* first searching Drive A, the default drive.)

7. Change the system prompt to display a message with the system date. Enter the following:

   `PROMPT It is $d$g What is your command?`

   Execute a few commands (such as DIR, VOL, and VER) to experience the new system prompt. Then return the system prompt back to its default by entering PROMPT NG.

8. Change the system prompt to display the current directory. Then change to several directories to see the effect:

   `A> PROMPT $P$G`

   `A> CD\WORD`

   `A> CD\LOTUS\CURR`

   `A> CD\`

9. Bonus Exercise:

   - Change the default disk to Drive A. Copy at least two files from the root directory of Drive A to the WORD directory created above.

   - Create a directory (TEMP) from the root directory of Drive A.

   - Change to TEMP, copy all files from A:\WORD to TEMP, and use the DIR command to verify the copy process. Use wildcard characters whenever possible to save keystrokes and minimize errors.

   - Finally, remove the TEMP directory and change back to the C> prompt. Did you remember to delete the files in TEMP first?

   This ends Chapter 4 lab exercises. Remove your disk when you are done, and remember, "practice is the best teacher."

Summary of Essential DOS Commands

The term filespec in the command formats below refers to the complete filename [d:][path]filename[.ext]. The optional parts of commands are shown in brackets and chapter references are shown in parentheses. External commands are indicated with an asterisk.

CD	[d:][path] Changes directories (4)
*CHKDSK	[d:][filespec] [/V] Checks status of a disk and RAM (3)
COPY	filespec [d:][filespec] Copies specified files (3)
DATE	[mm-dd-yy] -or- [mm/dd/yy] Displays and sets the system date (2)
DEL	filespec Deletes (erases) specified files (2)
DIR	[d:][filespec] [/P][/W] Displays directory entries (3)
*DISKCOPY	[d:[d:]] Makes an exact copy of a disk (3)
*FORMAT	[d:] [/S][/V] Formats a disk to receive DOS files (2)

MD	[d:]path Makes a new directory (4)
PATH	[d:][path][;path...] Sets a search path for executable files (4)
PROMPT	[text] Assigns the system prompt (4)
RENAME	filespec filename[.ext] Renames a file (3)
RD	[d:]path Removes a directory (4)
TIME	[hh:mm[:ss] Displays and sets the system time (2)
TYPE	filespec Displays the contents of a text file (2)
VER	Displays the DOS version number (3)

Common DOS Error Messages

Abort, Ignore, Retry, Fail?

A disk error has occurred. Enter A to end the process that requested the disk read or write operation. Enter R to retry the operation, or F to end the operation, but continue the process that requested the disk read or write. Entering I should be avoided because it can cause a loss of data. Early versions of DOS do not include the Fail option.

Abort, Retry, Fail?

A floppy disk device error has occurred. Normally you should enter R to try again after correcting the problem, usually by either closing the latch on the drive or reinserting the disk. If the second attempt fails, enter A to terminate the process.

Bad command or filename

The command entered is: (1) not a valid DOS command, (2) DOS cannot find the command, or (3) DOS cannot find a file specified. Often the correct path is not provided for DOS to locate the command or file.

Bad or missing Command Interpreter

COMMAND.COM is not on the root directory of the boot disk.

Disk error reading (or writing) drive x:

The disk in the specified drive has a bad sector. If entering R (retry) does not resolve the problem, enter A to end the process.

Disk unsuitable for system disk

FORMAT detected a bad track on the disk where system files reside. The disk can only be formatted as a non-system disk.

File cannot be copied onto itself

The source file name is the same as the target file name. Make sure the target file name (drive, path, etc.) is complete.

File creation error

You tried to add a file name that already exists in the directory, or there was not enough space for the file.

Format failure

A fatal disk error prevented DOS from formatting the disk.

Incorrect DOS version

You attempted to run a DOS command from a version of DOS that is different from the version used to boot the system. Reenter the DOS command from the DOS version used to boot the system.

Insufficient disk space

The disk does not contain enough room to perform the operation.

Invalid number of parameters

The command line entered did not contain the correct number of parameters for the command you invoked.

Invalid parameter(s)

One of the command options is wrong or does not exist.

Invalid path, not directory, or directory not empty

You could not remove a directory for one of the specified reasons. Correct the problem and reenter the command.

Non-system disk or disk error

Not a bootable DOS disk.

Not ready error reading drive x: Abort, Retry, Fail?

DOS cannot read or write to the specified drive. Make sure the drive latch is closed and that it contains a disk.

Program too big to fit in memory

DOS cannot load an executable program because of insufficient free space. Remove any unnecessary buffers and TSR programs.

Write protect error writing drive x:

You tried to write data to a disk with a write-protect tab covering the notch, or it does not have a write-protect notch.

Index

M

MD command, 42
MS-DOS, 2

O

Operating system, 1
Options for commands, 16
Organizing files, 40

P

Parking the heads, 39
Path, 41
PATH command, 44
Pause option, 16
PC-DOS, 2
PRN, 20
PROMPT command, 45

R

RAM (Random Access Memory), 4
RAM-resident programs, 4
RD command, 44
Record, 3
Redirection, 20
Removing directories, 44
RENAME command (REN), 33
Root directory, 40

S

Saving files, 3
Sector, 11
Slash, 16
Subdirectory, 40
System prompt, 6

T

TIME command, 19
Track, 11
TYPE command, 20

V

VER (Version) command, 34
Volume label, 12

W

Warm boot, 7
Wide option, 16
Wildcard characters, 17